I0426369

July 2012

INTERNATIONAL TAXATION

Information on Foreign-Owned but Essentially U.S.-Based Corporate Groups Is Limited

G A O

Accountability ★ Integrity ★ Reliability

Contents

Letter		1
	Scope and Methodology	2
	Summary	3
	Agency Comments	4
Appendix I	Briefing Slides	6

Abbreviations

FCDC	foreign-controlled domestic corporation
IRS	Internal Revenue Service
SOI	Statistics of Income

United States Government Accountability Office
Washington, DC 20548

July 16, 2012

The Honorable Max Baucus
Chairman
The Honorable Orrin G. Hatch
Ranking Member
Committee on Finance
United States Senate

A multinational corporate group, whether U.S.-owned or foreign-owned, with subsidiaries inside and outside of the United States can shift income to its subsidiaries in countries where corporate taxes are lower in order to avoid or evade U.S. taxes. As detailed in previous reports, this income shifting can be accomplished through such practices as manipulating transfer prices (the prices that members of the corporate group charge each other for goods and services).[1] Foreign-owned multinational corporations can do this even if the majority of their economic activity is in the United States. Tax policymakers have long been concerned about the tax compliance implications of these practices.

It is not clear what is known about foreign-parented corporate groups with U.S. subsidiaries where the majority of worldwide operations are in the United States. You asked us to provide information about corporate groups that fit this description. Specifically, we agreed to determine (1) whether there are advantages in this ownership structure for avoiding or evading taxes, and (2) what is known about the number, size, type, and other relevant characteristics of these corporate groups and how they came to be organized with this structure.

The enclosed slides (see app. I) compile and expand upon information previously presented to you in response to your request for information about certain foreign-owned but essentially U.S.-based corporate groups.

---

[1]See, for example, GAO, *International Taxation: Study Countries That Exempt Foreign-Source Income Face Compliance Risks and Burdens Similar to Those in the United States*, GAO-09-934 (Washington, DC.: Sept. 15, 2009); *International Taxation: Information on Federal Contractors With Offshore Subsidiaries*, GAO-04-293 (Washington, DC.: Feb. 2, 2004); and *International Taxation: Transfer Pricing and Information on Nonpayment of Tax*, GAO/GGD-95-101 (Washington, DC.: Apr. 13, 1995).

Scope and Methodology

To determine whether there are advantages in the foreign-controlled domestic corporation (FCDC)[2] ownership structure for avoiding or evading taxes,[3] we reviewed applicable laws and regulations and interviewed Internal Revenue Service (IRS) officials and academic experts.

To determine what is known about these corporate groups, we reviewed academic, government, and other research to find studies that reported on foreign-owned but essentially U.S.-based corporate groups. We used two methods to collect data on these multinational corporations. The first method used annual reports to compare U.S. sales[4] to the foreign parent company's worldwide sales to determine the U.S. share of worldwide operations. To implement this method, we took a sample of 100 corporations identified as large FCDCs from the IRS's Statistics of Income files on corporate tax returns for tax year 2007. We matched these FCDCs to their ultimate owners[5] using Nexis and annual reports. For these ultimate owners that broke out U.S. sales separately in their annual reports, we calculated the U.S. share of worldwide operations by dividing the U.S. sales by the worldwide sales. The second method used the country of the foreign parent company's principal business activity as an indicator of whether the parent company had the majority of its operations in the United States. To implement this method, we identified the ultimate owners as the ultimate shareholder of the FCDC as reported on IRS Form 5472.[6] We counted the foreign parent companies and

---

[2]For purposes of this report, a FCDC is a U.S. corporation with 50 percent or more of its voting stock owned directly or indirectly by a foreign person or entity.

[3]Tax avoidance is the legal practice of reducing taxes owed through such means as taking legitimate deductions. Tax evasion, on the other hand, is the illegal practice of willfully not paying taxes owed by such means as claiming deductions to which one is not entitled.

[4]We use the term "sales" to represent sales or gross receipts on a tax return, or sales or revenue on an income statement.

[5]For the purposes of this report, we are using the term "ultimate owner" in two different contexts. When applying our first method, we use ultimate owner to mean the ultimate foreign parents identified using Nexis, corporate websites, and annual reports without regard to the percentage of ownership or other possible owners. In this context, each FCDC corresponds with a single ultimate owner. When applying our second method, ultimate owner means the ultimate indirect 25 percent foreign shareholder whose ownership of stock is not attributable to any other 25 percent foreign shareholder, as reported on the Form 5472. In this context an FCDC may have multiple ultimate owners.

[6]Form 5472 is entitled "Information Return of a 25% Foreign-Owned U.S. Corporation or a Foreign Corporation Engaged in a U.S. Trade or Business."

attempted to identify their principal business activity country for all large FCDCs that filed Form 5472 in 2008. Also, for this objective, we reviewed foreign parent company annual reports and expert studies on how these FCDCs become foreign-owned to describe what is known about the ways in which they came to be organized as foreign-owned but essentially U.S.-based corporate groups.

We conducted this work from July 2011 to July 2012 in accordance with generally accepted government auditing standards. Those standards require that we plan and perform the audit to obtain sufficient, appropriate evidence to provide a reasonable basis for our findings and conclusions based on our audit objectives. We believe that the evidence obtained provides a reasonable basis for our findings based on our audit objectives.

Summary

The FCDC ownership structure could provide a tax avoidance or evasion advantage relative to a structure where U.S. parents own foreign subsidiaries. Academic experts we spoke to said that the FCDC corporate structure does not provide an inherently greater ability to evade taxes through transfer pricing abuse because transfer pricing rules are the same for the FCDC structure as for U.S. corporations with foreign subsidiaries. However, according to IRS officials and our own research, the FCDC structure could confer a tax advantage because certain rules that can limit potential abuse by U.S. parent companies and their foreign subsidiaries may not apply to FCDCs and their foreign parent companies. These rules (called anti-deferral rules) make immediately taxable to U.S. corporations certain types of income such as interest, rents, and royalties of their foreign subsidiaries. These types of income tend to be easily moveable from one taxing jurisdiction to another and hence more amenable to transfer pricing abuse.

Very little is known about the foreign parents of corporations with a majority of their operations in the United States. Studies of this corporate structure were limited to studies of corporations that inverted to achieve this structure. In an inversion, a corporate group with a U.S. owner typically creates a new foreign corporation in a low tax country that becomes the foreign owner of the corporate group in order to reduce the group's tax liabilities. Even in these cases, the studies did not claim to have information on all inversions. Our own attempts to identify foreign parents of corporations with a majority of their operations in the United States ran into important limitations. In our first method—comparing U.S. sales to the foreign parent's worldwide sales as shown on their annual reports—provided unrepresentative results because too few foreign parents broke out U.S. sales separately. In addition, results from our second method—using the country where the foreign parent's principal business activities were located (as reported on IRS Form 5472)—were difficult because IRS does not define principal countries where business is conducted on the form, allowing taxpayers to claim more than one country as a principal location where business is conducted. Thus, the information on the form does not permit clear inferences about how much business the foreign-controlled corporate group does in any particular country, including the United States. Without basic information about these foreign-owned but essentially U.S.-based corporate groups, describing how they came to adopt this structure is not feasible. The benefits of obtaining more information about the possible effects on tax compliance of these foreign-controlled corporate groups, other characteristics of the corporate groups and how they came to be organized as they are would have to be weighed against the cost of collecting such data.

Agency Comments

The IRS provided technical comments after viewing a draft of this report, which we incorporated as appropriate.

As agreed with your offices, unless you publicly announce the contents of this report earlier, we plan no further distribution until 30 days from the date of this letter. At that time, we will send copies to interested congressional committees, the Secretary of the Treasury, the Commissioner of Internal Revenue, and other interested parties. Copies are also available at no charge on the GAO website at http://www.gao.gov.

Should you or your staff have questions concerning this report, please contact me at (202) 512-9110 or whitej@gao.gov. Key contributors to this report were Kevin Daly, Assistant Director; Susan Baker; JoAnna Berry;

Emily Gruenwald; George Guttman; Laurie King; Ed Nannenhorn; Karen O'Conor; Cynthia Saunders; and Andrew Stephens.

James R. White

James R. White
Director, Tax Issues
Strategic Issues

Appendix I: Briefing Slides

International Taxation:

Information on Foreign-Owned but Essentially U.S.-Based Corporate Groups Is Limited

Introduction

- Foreign-parented groups with U.S. subsidiaries, like other multinational corporations, may engage in income shifting to low tax jurisdictions in order to avoid or evade U.S taxes.

    - A multinational corporate group, whether U.S. owned or foreign owned, may have subsidiaries in countries outside the United States where corporate tax rates may be lower.

    - This corporate structure can provide scope for income shifting through such practices as manipulation of transfer prices—the prices that members of the corporate group charge each other for goods and services—as detailed in prior GAO work.[1]

- Some of these multinationals—it is not clear how many—are foreign-parented corporate groups with U.S. subsidiaries whose U.S. operations constitute the majority of the group's worldwide operations.

[1]GAO, *International Taxation: Study Countries That Exempt Foreign- Source Income Face Compliance Risks and Burdens Similar to Those in the United States,* GAO-09-934 (Washington, DC.: Sept. 15, 2009); *International Taxation: Information on Federal Contractors With Offshore Subsidiaries,* GAO-04-293 (Washington, DC.: Feb. 2, 2004); and *International Taxation: Transfer Pricing and Information on Nonpayment of Tax,* GAO/GGD-95-101 (Washington, DC.: Apr. 13, 1995).

2

Objectives

- Because much is uncertain about these foreign-owned but essentially U.S.-based corporate groups, GAO agreed to determine:
  - whether there are advantages in this ownership structure for avoiding or evading taxes, and
  - what is known about the number, size, type, and other relevant characteristics of these corporate groups and how they came to be organized with this structure.

3

Scope and Methodology

Objective 1

- To determine whether there are advantages in the foreign-controlled domestic corporation (FCDC) ownership structure for avoiding or evading taxes, we interviewed Internal Revenue Service (IRS) officials and academic experts, and reviewed applicable laws and regulations.

Objective 2

- We reviewed academic, government, and other research to find studies that reported on multinational corporations with FCDCs whose operations were the majority of the multinational's worldwide operations.

- To count these multinational corporations, we used two methods for identifying which foreign parents of U.S. subsidiaries had the majority of their operations in the United States. The first method compared U.S. sales to the foreign parent's worldwide sales using annual reports to determine the U.S. share of operations. To implement this method:

    - We took a sample of 100 corporations identified as large FCDCs[1] from the IRS's Statistics of Income (SOI) files on corporate tax returns for tax year 2007.

    - We then used Nexis, corporate websites, and annual reports where available to match the FCDCs to their ultimate foreign parents which we will refer to as ultimate owners.

    - Of the corporations that we were able to match, we identified those that reported their worldwide sales in their annual reports.

---

[1]For purposes of this report, a large FCDC has at least $250 million of assets or at least $50 million of sales under this method.

4

Scope and Methodology (cont.)

- For these ultimate owners that broke out U.S. sales separately in their annual reports, we calculated the U.S. share of worldwide operations by dividing the U.S. sales by the worldwide sales as given in the annual reports.
  - To evaluate a possible alternative to this method, we also calculated the U.S. shares of worldwide operations for these corporations by dividing sales as reported on the FCDC's tax return by worldwide sales from the ultimate owner's annual report and compared the percentages.
- The second method used the country or countries identified as the principal places the foreign parent conducted business as an indicator of whether the parent had the majority of its operations in the United States. To implement this method:
  - We counted the ultimate owners and attempted to identify their principal business activity country using IRS data on transactions between all large FCDCs[1] that filed Form 5472 (Information Return of a 25% Foreign-Owned U.S. Corporation or a Foreign Corporation Engaged in a U.S. Trade or Business) and their related parties.
  - IRS officials told us that Form 5472 is used by IRS to obtain information on related party transactions and to identify potential transfer pricing abuses during examinations. The FCDC is not required to file Form 5472 annually—the form is filed only when the FCDC has reportable transactions.[2]

---

[1]For purposes of this report, a large FCDC has at least $500 million in total receipts under his method.
[2]Reportable transactions are those described on Form 5472 and include transactions between the FCDC and related parties made for monetary considerations such as sales, rents, etc., but also for nonmonetary considerations.

5

Scope and Methodology (cont.)

- The SOI Corporate File is a stratified sample of corporate tax returns that is often used for research purposes.
  - To ensure reliability, IRS performs a number of quality control steps to verify the internal consistency of its data such as computerized tests to verify the relationships between values on the returns.
  - We also conducted several reliability tests to ensure that the data excerpts we used for this report were complete and accurate, including a comparison of IRS published data to our computations to ensure that the data set was complete.
  - To ensure accuracy, we reviewed related documentation and electronically tested for errors. We concluded that the data were sufficiently reliable for the purposes of this report.

6

Summary

- Academic experts we spoke to said that the FCDC corporate structure does not provide an inherently greater ability to evade taxes through transfer pricing abuse because transfer pricing rules are the same for the FCDC structure as for U.S. corporations with foreign subsidiaries. However, the FCDC structure may provide an advantage because anti-deferral tax rules which backstop the transfer pricing regime by limiting tax advantages from income shifting for U.S. parent corporations may not apply to FCDCs and their foreign parents.

- Very little is known about these foreign-owned but essentially U.S.-based corporate groups and how they came to adopt this structure.
    - Studies have focused on corporations that inverted to achieve this structure. In an inversion, a corporate group with a U.S. owner typically creates a new foreign corporation in a low tax country that becomes the foreign owner of the corporate group in order to reduce the group's tax liabilities. The studies did not claim to have information on all such inversions.
    - Annual reports did not provide sufficient data for the sample of FCDCs to be representative of all large foreign-controlled domestic corporations. Too few foreign parents had publicly available annual reports, and of those that did, too few broke out U.S. sales separately.
    - Tax information from Form 5472 does not provide reliable information about U.S. sales or other indicators of the U.S. share of worldwide operations for these corporate groups. IRS does not define "principal country(ies) where business is conducted" on the form and taxpayers can claim more than one country as a principal location where business is conducted.
        - However, this analysis did reveal that large FCDCs generally were part of a complex worldwide corporate structure involving many related parties.
    - The absence of basic information about foreign-controlled corporate groups with the majority of their operations in the United States makes describing how they came to adopt such a structure infeasible.

- The benefits of obtaining more information about these corporate groups, how they came to be organized as they are, and the possible effects on tax compliance would have to be weighed against the cost of collecting this data.

7

FCDCs May Have a Tax Avoidance and Evasion Advantage Relative to U.S. Corporations with Foreign Subsidiaries

- According to IRS officials and our own research, FCDCs may have an advantage because anti-deferral rules that can limit potential abuse by U.S. parents and their foreign subsidiaries may not apply to FCDCs and their foreign parents.
  - Academic experts we spoke to said that the FCDC corporate structure is not inherently advantageous relative to a U.S. corporation with foreign subsidiaries in terms of greater ability to shift income through transfer pricing abuse to avoid paying U.S. taxes. The same rules for determining the appropriate transfer price would apply under both structures.
  - However, there are also anti-deferral rules that require U.S. parents to report currently (i.e., not defer reporting until the income is repatriated) certain types of income (called Subpart F income) earned by their controlled foreign corporations (CFC).[1] This income includes interest, rents, and royalties and other types of income that tend to be easily moveable from one taxing jurisdiction to another.
    - These anti-deferral rules do not apply to an FCDC unless it is also the owner of a CFC or to the foreign parent of an FCDC unless the foreign parent is itself a CFC.
  - These rules provide a backstop for the transfer pricing regime that limits income shifting for U.S. parent corporations that may not apply to FCDCs and their foreign parents.

---

[1]An entity is a CFC if "U.S. shareholders" own more than 50 percent of the total combined voting power of its stock or more than 50 percent of the stock's total value. To be considered a "U.S. shareholder" for the purposes of this definition, a U.S. person must own at least 10 percent of the total combined voting power of the corporation's stock. In calculating ownership, the statute considers direct, indirect, and constructive ownership. 26 U.S.C. §§ 951, 957.

8

No Comprehensive Studies of Foreign-Owned but Essentially U.S.-Based Corporate Groups Were Found

- Studies of foreign corporations with a majority of operations in the United States were few and not comprehensive.
  - The studies that have been done on this corporate structure focused on inversions—a practice where, typically, a corporate group with a U.S. owner creates a new foreign corporation in a low tax country that becomes the foreign owner of the corporate group in order to reduce the group's tax liabilities.
  - These studies analyzed a relative handful of corporations and did not claim to have information on all inversions.

9

For Our Sample, Not All Ultimate Owners Could Be Identified and Few Broke Out U.S. Sales

- As table 1 shows, of the 100 large FCDCs sampled, we identified 85 ultimate owners.
- We found annual reports for 63 of these ultimate owners that provided worldwide sales.
  - Of these 63 ultimate owners, 20 broke out U.S. and worldwide sales separately.
  - Of the 20 ultimate owners, 16 were foreign.
- There were 22 annual reports we could not find; all were private corporations.

10

Analysis of the Sample of 100 FCDCs

Table 1: Number of Ultimate Owners by Country and Availability of Sales Amounts from 2007 Sample

Ultimate owners	Foreign ultimate owner		U.S. ultimate owner[1]		Ultimate owner unknown	Total
Number of ultimate owners by country for the sample of 100 large FCDCs	73		12		15	100
	Public	Private	Public	Private		
Number of ultimate owners that were public or private	53	20[2]	4	8[3]		85
Number of ultimate owners that identified worldwide sales in annual reports	53	6	4	0		63
Number of ultimate owners that broke out U.S. sales from worldwide sales	14	2	4	0		20

Source: GAO analysis of IRS data and ultimate owner information.

[1]A FCDC can have a U.S. ultimate owner when the FCDC's foreign parent is a corporation that is owned by a U.S. corporation.
[2]Of these 20 foreign private ultimate owners, 14 were identified using 2012 Nexis and corporate website information and 6 using annual reports with 2007 sales amounts.
[3]All 8 of these U.S. private ultimate owners were identified using 2012 Nexis and corporate website informa ion.

11

Annual Report Data in the Sample Was Not Representative of the FCDCs' Foreign-Controlled Corporate Groups

- As figure 1 shows, of the 16 foreign ultimate owners that broke out U.S. sales, there were 6 foreign corporations that had at least 50 percent of worldwide sales in the United States.

    - Annual reports did not provide sufficient data for the sample of FCDCs to be representative of all large foreign-controlled domestic corporations. Too few foreign ultimate owners had publicly available annual reports, and of those that did, too few broke out U.S. sales separately.

- An additional limitation to this analysis is that differences in accounting standards and methods across countries may make some of the percentages hard to compare. For example, differences in when income is recognized might make the percentages higher or lower.

- Because so few foreign ultimate owners broke out U.S. sales, it was not worthwhile to attempt to adjust for these accounting differences across countries.

12

U.S. Share of Foreign Ultimate Owner's Worldwide Sales from Annual Report Data

Figure 1: U.S. Sales as Percentage of Worldwide Sales for the Foreign Ultimate Owners Reporting U.S. Sales Separately (unadjusted for accounting differences)

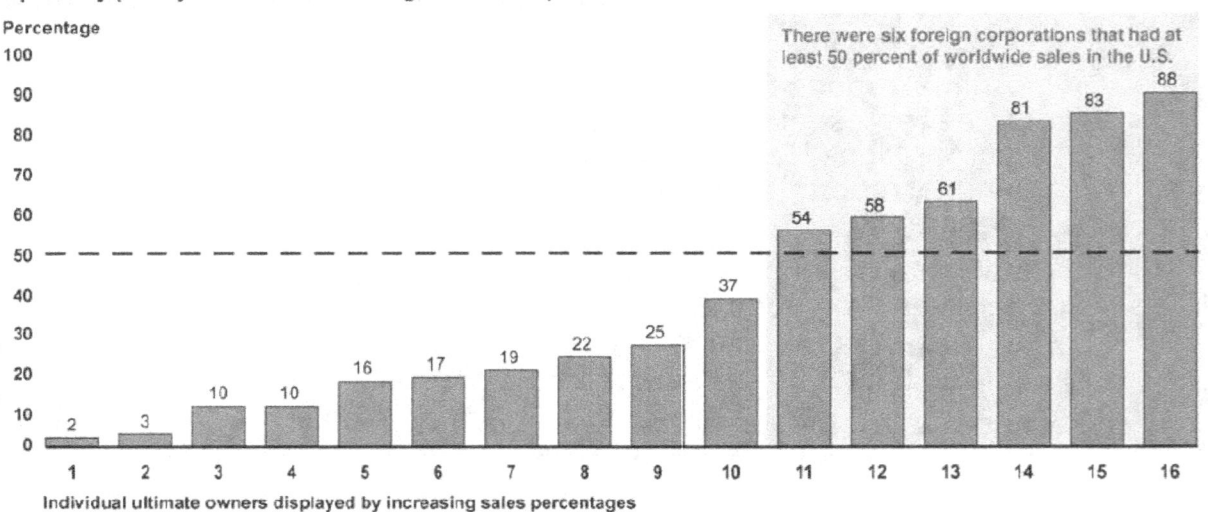

Source: GAO analysis of foreign ultimate owner annual reports.

Note: These amounts were not adjusted for accounting differences across countries.

13

Sales Data from Tax Returns Are Not Reliable Substitutes for Missing Annual Report Sales Data

- We explored the alternative of using the FCDCs' U.S. sales as reported on their tax returns as a substitute for the missing U.S. sales when these are not broken out in annual reports.
  - In these cases, the U.S. share of worldwide sales would be calculated by dividing U.S. sales from FCDCs' tax returns by the foreign corporate groups' worldwide sales from annual reports.
- However, as figure 2 shows, for the 16 cases where the alternatives could be directly compared because the ultimate owner broke out U.S. sales on its annual report, there were some wide differences in the U.S. share of worldwide sales.
  - The figure shows the percentage point difference when the U.S. share of worldwide sales using annual report data is compared to the U.S. share using information from the FCDC's tax return.[1]
  - This difference (in absolute value) was 25 percent or more for 6 of the ultimate owners and for 4 of these, the difference was 50 percent or more.
- These differences arise from limitations which may cause the shares to be higher or lower in an unpredictable way such as:
  - differences in accounting standards that exist across countries, differences between income recognized for accounting and tax purposes, differences in reporting periods for the FCDC and ultimate owner, and the ultimate owner not identifying consolidated subsidiaries in its annual report.
- In addition, the limitations may cause the shares to be predictably higher or lower such as when:
  - the ultimate owner may own multiple FCDCs (including some not in our sample) or have U.S. sales not attributable to any FCDC which could cause our sample's FCDC's sales to be less than the worldwide group's U.S. sales, and the FCDC may have sales made outside the United States, as these non-U.S. sales are generally considered taxable income, which could cause the FCDC's sales to be greater than the worldwide group's U.S. sales.

[1]The percentage point difference is equal to (annual report U.S. sales/annual report worldwide sales) minus (tax return U.S. sales/annual report worldwide sales).

14

Comparison of the U.S. Share of Worldwide Sales Using Annual Report and Tax Return Data

Figure 2: U.S. Shares of Ultimate Owners' Worldwide Sales from Annual Reports Minus U.S Share of Ultimate Owners' Worldwide Sales from Tax Returns[1]

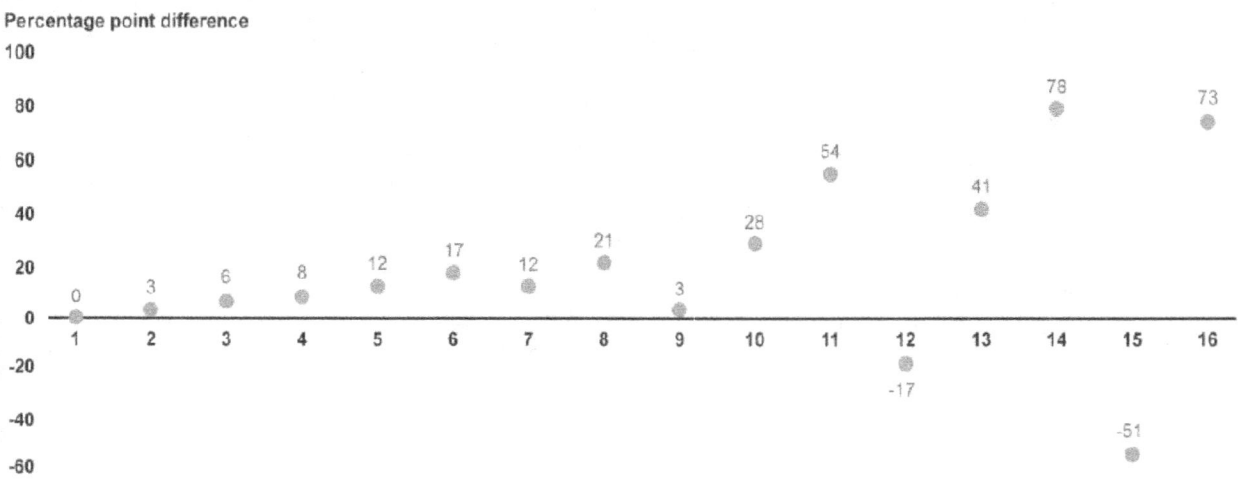

Percentage point difference

Individual ultimate owners (displayed in same order as Figure 1)

Source: GAO analysis of foreign ultimate owner annual reports and IRS data.

[1]Negative differences are corporations where he FCDC's U.S. sales on its tax return are greater han the ultimate owner's U.S. sales on its annual report.

15

IRS Form 5472 Cannot Be Used To Get Information about the U.S. Share of the Ultimate Owners' Worldwide Operations

- IRS does not define "principal country(ies) where business is conducted" on the form and taxpayers can claim more than one country as a principal location where business is conducted.
  - Taxpayers are instructed on Form 5472 to provide the principal country or countries where business is conducted.
  - However, the instructions do not define "principal country(ies) where business is conducted" and permits taxpayers to list more than one country where business is conducted.
  - Given these limitations of Form 5472, it is not possible to determine the percentage of worldwide business in a particular country or whether the business represents a majority of the ultimate owner's worldwide business.
  - Changes to the form in order to better identify the foreign corporations with majority operations in the United States would have to be assessed according to their full cost and benefits. The changes could impact a wide range of activities within IRS from compliance to returns processing.

- However, as figure 3 shows, aspects of the organizational structure can be inferred from information available on the Form 5472.
  - The chart shows the ultimate parties in each relationship. Intermediate parties may exist that complicate the structure and Form 5472 generally does not contain information on these intermediates.

16

Corporate Group Structure Based on Form 5472 Information

Figure 3: Potential Relationships between FCDCs and Related Parties[1]

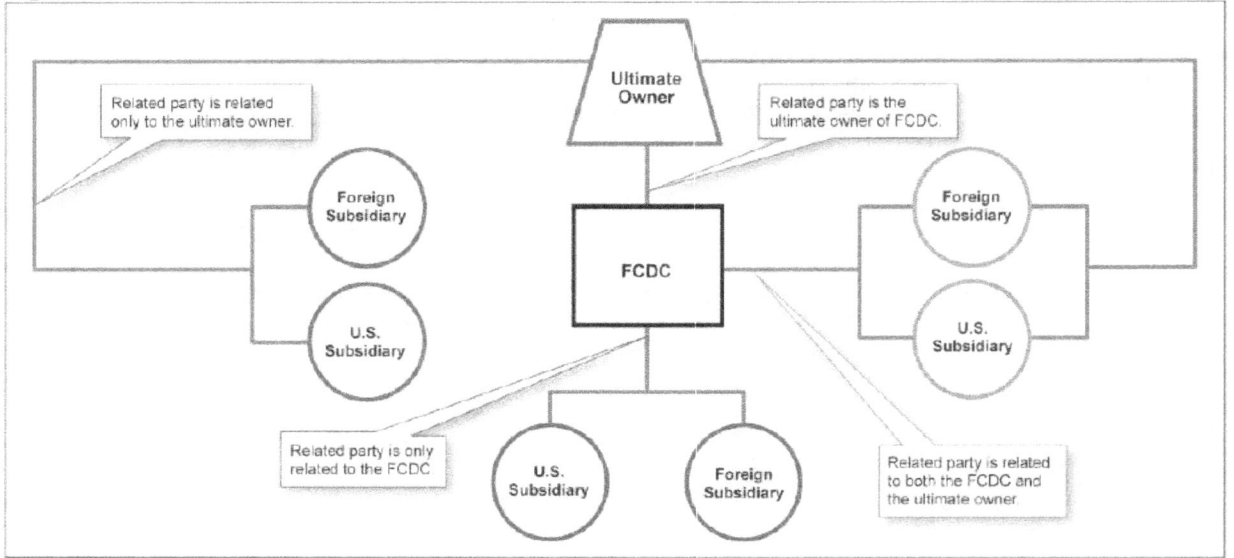

Source: GAO analysis of IRS data.

[1]The lines indicate an ownership relationship. The chart identifies related parties as corporations for simplicity. Other types of entities such as partnerships may also be related parties.

17

Large FCDCs Generally Were Part of a Complex Worldwide Corporate Structure

- In 2008, large FCDCs had transactions with many related parties with different ownership relationships to the FCDC.
    - As figure 4 shows, there were 971 unique large FCDCs that had 2,356 ultimate owners.[1]
    - The FCDCs had transactions with 31,676 other members of the worldwide corporate group, of which 28,442 were foreign.[2]

[1]The ultimate owner is identified from Form 5472 as the ultimate indirect 25 percent foreign shareholder whose ownership of stock is not attributable to any other 25 percent foreign shareholder.

[2]There were 2,792 related par ies that were recorded as both U.S. and foreign persons and seven related parties that did not identify their corporate relationship. IRS provided a formula to use for characterizing the parties that reported as both foreign and United States.

18

Corporate Group Structure with Number of Related Parties in 2008

Figure 4: Number of Related Parties Having Transactions with Large FCDCs in 2008[1]

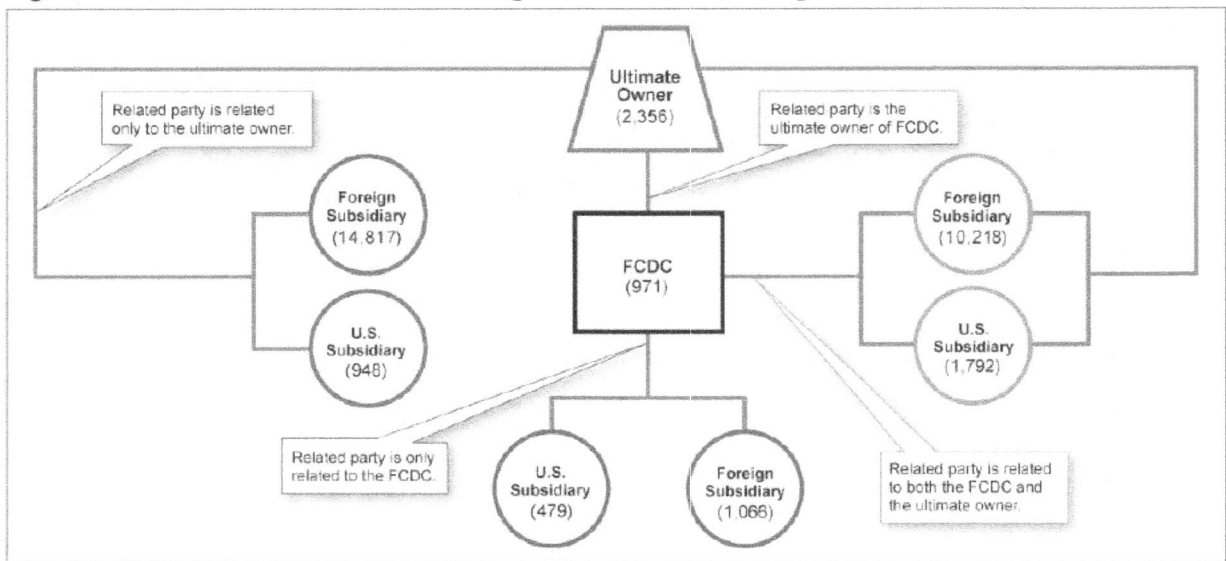

Source: GAO analysis of IRS data.

[1]The organizational chart shows the number of related parties, identified as foreign or U.S. persons, with reportable transactions between the corporate entities as shown in figure 3. However, the ultimate owners include both foreign and U.S. persons—2,341 were identified as foreign and 15 as United States. These descriptions are derived from Form 5472, Section III. Data are taken from the 2008 5472 SOI sample file for large FCDCs.

19

Lack of Basic Information Makes Determining How the Corporate Groups Became Foreign-Owned Infeasible

- The absence of basic information about foreign-controlled corporate groups with the majority of their operations in the United States makes describing how they came to adopt such a structure infeasible.
    - In our sample, annual reports did not generally provide the method used by the FCDCs to become foreign-owned.
- Studies show that foreign ownership can occur in a number of ways, such as:
    - inversions by corporations reincorporating or restructuring in foreign countries,
    - takeovers or mergers by foreign corporations,
    - foreign corporations with U.S. subsidiaries incorporating overseas at the onset, or
    - foreign corporations expanding their operations and establishing new subsidiaries in the United States.
- However, since there is no basic information about these foreign-controlled corporate groups, there is no way to determine how often they may choose these different ways to become foreign-owned.
- As in the case of identifying these corporations through a revision of IRS's Form 5472, the benefits of obtaining a better understanding of how they came to be organized as they are would have to be weighed against the cost of collecting this information.

20

GAO's Mission	The Government Accountability Office, the audit, evaluation, and investigative arm of Congress, exists to support Congress in meeting its constitutional responsibilities and to help improve the performance and accountability of the federal government for the American people. GAO examines the use of public funds; evaluates federal programs and policies; and provides analyses, recommendations, and other assistance to help Congress make informed oversight, policy, and funding decisions. GAO's commitment to good government is reflected in its core values of accountability, integrity, and reliability.
Obtaining Copies of GAO Reports and Testimony	The fastest and easiest way to obtain copies of GAO documents at no cost is through GAO's website (www.gao.gov). Each weekday afternoon, GAO posts on its website newly released reports, testimony, and correspondence. To have GAO e-mail you a list of newly posted products, go to www.gao.gov and select "E-mail Updates."
Order by Phone	The price of each GAO publication reflects GAO's actual cost of production and distribution and depends on the number of pages in the publication and whether the publication is printed in color or black and white. Pricing and ordering information is posted on GAO's website, http://www.gao.gov/ordering.htm.
	Place orders by calling (202) 512-6000, toll free (866) 801-7077, or TDD (202) 512-2537.
	Orders may be paid for using American Express, Discover Card, MasterCard, Visa, check, or money order. Call for additional information.
Connect with GAO	Connect with GAO on Facebook, Flickr, Twitter, and YouTube. Subscribe to our RSS Feeds or E-mail Updates. Listen to our Podcasts. Visit GAO on the web at www.gao.gov.
To Report Fraud, Waste, and Abuse in Federal Programs	Contact: Website: www.gao.gov/fraudnet/fraudnet.htm E-mail: fraudnet@gao.gov Automated answering system: (800) 424-5454 or (202) 512-7470
Congressional Relations	Katherine Siggerud, Managing Director, siggerudk@gao.gov, (202) 512-4400, U.S. Government Accountability Office, 441 G Street NW, Room 7125, Washington, DC 20548
Public Affairs	Chuck Young, Managing Director, youngc1@gao.gov, (202) 512-4800 U.S. Government Accountability Office, 441 G Street NW, Room 7149 Washington, DC 20548

Please Print on Recycled Paper.